MW00529573

Over a long and rich ca[...]
to and transcendent of any vogue—has persisted in addressing what I can only and inadequately label matters of the spirit. He'd surely be the last earthly soul to celebrate the death of a beloved son, "who is both not here, and not not here," as occasion for his most powerful work to date. And yet it is that. And it *is* spiritual. To read *In the Unwalled City* is to have our hearts broken, poem after poem, even as *we* celebrate the deeper-than-deep humanity of its testimony. I'm simply aware of no recent poetry that matches it for mournful eloquence.

—Sydney Lea,
Author of *Here*, former Poet Laureate of Vermont

In a grieving father's voice, both vulnerable and steeled, the poet writes, "My son is dead and done with me." He talks to himself through hybrid prose and poetry and to himself while talking to his son and, almost as afterthought, to us. He avails himself (and his off-camera readers) of centuries of wisdom, but, mercifully, offers us no moral *summas* gleaned from his devastating experience. Cording's bracing metaphors and sudden shifts of perspective distinguish *In the Unwalled City* from many memoirs of grief and loss. We come to poetry for just this: intimacy and awakening.

—Martha Serpas,
Author of *Double Effect*

Throughout Robert Cording's *In the Unwalled City*, one is immersed in the essence of duality—first, in a mingling of memoir and lyric—where language itself is an incantatory talisman against incredible loss yet unable to offer lasting solace. The title essay and collection of linked poems concerning the poet's late son impart a gorgeous grief which simultaneously embraces remembrance while also seeking some means of forgetfulness at "an altar where all rationality had to be sacrificed."

—**Claude Wilkinson**,
Author of *World Without End*

Every loss is particular; each bereavement has its own indigenous flavor. In this book of prose memoir and poetry, Robert Cording offers us an especially open and personal chronicle of grieving, generous in its detail, unsparing in its honest accounting of his own helplessness and "notknowing." Grief is work in the dark, and it allows for no easy or even orthodox comfort. Because Cording accepts his new and stark vulnerability, the intimacy of the poems deepens as he labors to remain conversant with his son and not lose his "fatherhood." By remaining present to what is no longer present, over time the grieving father uncovers gifts of mercy and gratitude. And if Cording captures, over and over, how the ordinary and daily can be harrowing in its impact, *In the Unwalled City* is essentially a gentle, probing book—an uneasy elegy, a tribute to abiding love.

—**Margaret Gibson**,
Author of *The Glass Globe*, Poet Laureate of Connecticut

Robert Cording's heartbreaking book, *In the Unwalled City*, explores a terrible loss—the death of his son Daniel from an accidental overdose of opioids—with uncommon tenderness and grace. "Lord, grant me this fatherhood of pain," he writes, "do not let grief be finished with me, // if only because it gives birth to my dead son, / who is both not here, and not not here." He gazes steadily into this void, discovering not only a language for his grief but the saving power of love, which shines forth on every page. This is a book for the ages.

—Christopher Merrill,
Author of *Self-Portrait with Dogwood*

IN THE
UNWALLED
CITY

Books by Robert Cording

Poetry
Life-list (1987)
What Binds Us to This World (1991)
Heavy Grace (1996)
Against Consolation (2001)
Common Life (2006)
Walking With Ruskin (2010)
A Word in My Mouth: Selected Spiritual Poems (2013)
Only So Far (2015)
Without My Asking (2019)

Prose
Finding the World's Fullness (2019)

Edited
In My Life: Encounters with the Beatles (1998)
(eds: Cording, Jankowski-Smith, Miller-Laino)

IN THE
UNWALLED
CITY

ROBERT CORDING

SL/\NT

B O O K S

IN THE UNWALLED CITY

Copyright © 2022 Robert Cording. All rights reserved. Except for brief
quotations in critical publications or reviews, no part of this book may be re-
produced in any manner without prior written permission from the publisher.
Write: Permissions, Slant Books, P.O. Box 60295, Seattle, WA 98160.

Slant Books
P.O. Box 60295
Seattle, WA 98160

www.slantbooks.com

HARDCOVER ISBN: 978-1-63982-115-0
PAPERBACK ISBN: 978-1-63982-114-3
EBOOK ISBN: 978-1-63982-115-0

Cataloguing-in-Publication data:

Names: Cording, Robert.

Title: In the unwalled city / Robert Cording.

Description: Seattle, WA: Slant Books, 2022.

Identifiers: ISBN 978-1-63982-115-0 (hardcover) |ISBN 978-1-63982-114-3 (paperback)
| ISBN 978-1-63982-115-0 (ebook)

Subjects: LCSH: American poetry -- 21st century | Grief -- Poetry | Bereavement
-- Poetry | Death -- Poetry

Classification: CALL NUMBER PS3553.O6455 I53 2022 (paperback) | PS3553.O6455
I53 2022 (ebook)

For Daniel

If I did not believe in the comfort of the spirit;
if your presence, which I cannot locate anywhere
other than myself, did not still console,
I might have no reason for talking to you
as if you were alive,
for constantly going out to you in these words
as if you could receive them.

Contents

III

IV

The sorrow for the dead is the only sorrow from which we refuse to be divorced. Every other wound we seek to heal, every other affliction to forget; but this wound we consider it a duty to keep open; this affliction we cherish and brood over in solitude.

—Washington Irving

. . . you *must* continue his life inside of yours insofar as it has been unfinished; his life has now passed onto yours.

—Rilke, **Letter to Sidonie Nádherná von Borutín**

IN THE UNWALLED CITY (1)

Against other things it is possible to obtain security, but when it comes to death, we human beings all live in an unwalled city.

—Epicurus

IN THE EARLY HOURS of October 14, 2017, my wife's cell phone rang. The call was from my son Daniel's wife, Leisl, who could hardly speak, but managed "I need you and Bob to come home right now." My wife—not in response to Leisl, but to what she already knew as death's sudden assault, cried out, "No, no, no, no." Then I was talking—to the EMT, Peter, whom I knew from ushering at church. The emergency squad, he told me, was administering CPR to my son, but it "didn't look good."

We were in the Adirondacks. Daniel and Leisl lived in Woodstock, Connecticut, where my wife and I also live. Halfway across the Massachusetts Turnpike, I realized what Peter meant: that my son was already dead when he arrived. Two hours later, no one had called back to say Daniel had been taken to a hospital. I asked my wife if she thought our son was dead. She said yes.

I begin here. I have written at least four other beginnings. But there is no beginning. I say to myself, Daniel died. Daniel is dead. But his death goes on living, goes on requiring some response.

With grief one day becomes another. Every tomorrow repeats today, every day repeats itself. Grief can also be a sudden assault—images of Daniel cuddling the cats that seemed to occupy our house for years; Daniel, maybe eight years old, climbing out his window and walking around the scaffolding we had erected to clapboard our house and knocking on our bedroom window; or later (I must grieve it seems every aspect of my son's life, from child to adult), Daniel as a surly teenager who smoked too much pot and fought with me about everything; who sprawled in the back seat of the car, pushing his two brothers into one another; or most recently, Daniel, completely at home at the top of a forty foot ladder or pushing snow from a condo unit's high roof by sliding down its steep incline and letting the snow build up before him to bring him to a stop; Daniel who could focus on the job at hand so well, all else simply vanished. I wander, round and round, my days punctuated only by these sudden stabs of memory.

Daniel was thirty-one when he died. Writing about one's child is like writing about one's parents—it cannot help but be bewildering and fraudulent. It is a task that inevitably smooths out all the unknown and unknowable jagged edges.

I knew my son well. I didn't know him at all. Every parent can say the same. Since Daniel died, I have often wondered if his death would be more bearable if we really knew each other, if there wasn't the always unfinished business of coming-to-know.

Thankfully, Daniel was my Shakespearean fool: when it seemed to him that I was simplifying his life or life in general, or entertaining some impossible yearning as I just did in the paragraph above, he would usually sing out, *La, la . . . la, la*—kindly but mockingly, his nonsense for my nonsense.

I'd like to say: "I am writing now to make my son live again." That's true, of course, in the sense that all writing is an act of resurrection, or simply a means in my case of preventing Daniel from vanishing as if he had never been. But I am also writing, in part, to get back my real life. Grief involves a double loss—first, my loved son; and then my own life, at least as I knew it.

I have difficulty remembering what my life was like before Daniel died. I don't feel those constant memories of all that has been taken away. "Before" for me doesn't involve some loss of what I was or had. But I do feel that sense of everything suddenly being entirely and surreally different.

After Daniel died, I placed a photograph of him on my desk. In it, we are sitting in beach chairs parallel to one another on the Woodstock town beach. We are both in sunglasses looking at the water. I am in my forties. Daniel is seven or eight. When I put this photograph on my desk, I could only bear photographs of Daniel as a child. They consoled, not because they expressed the innocent joys of childhood, but because they were already-lived moments, finished moments of his life. This was Daniel at eight. This was him at twelve. At fourteen. They helped me believe, as I wanted to believe, that every life, no matter how shortened, is a complete life.

When I was in graduate school, I felt the immense gulf between the consolations of religion and the actual grief of a father in Ben Jonson's poem, "On My First Son." Jonson begins with a stoic "Farewell, thou child of my right hand" and reminds the reader that our children's lives are not ours to keep, but gifts that are lent to us by God. Jonson's "sin" is "too much hope of thee, lov'd boy," a hope that fostered his illusion that his son's life was guaranteed to go on longer than his own. And then the poet offers up all the usual consolations: that his son has escaped the "world's and flesh's rage," and even escaped the indignities and sufferings of growing old.

But at the poem's center is Jonson's inescapable grief that arrives, as if involuntarily, in this outburst: "O, could I lose all father now!" That "could" announces what cannot be escaped—the flesh and blood of fatherhood, the lost flesh and blood of one's child.

I have been reading Dante lately, and I have thought about his *Paradiso* and imagined how, if I came upon my son, he'd be a ray or orb of light, but he wouldn't be in his body. I know, from Dante's perspective, the resurrection of the body has yet to take place. But, forgive me, what I want is what Jonson wanted—my son in his body, still full of the "flesh's rage."

The medieval Jewish rabbi Nachmanides said, when "a man's child dies, it is fitting that he, and those that love him, grieve and mourn—but their mourning must be such that it is in service of the Lord." Though each day my son dies over and over, I turn and turn to the idea that gratitude is necessary for what was, even in the midst of the pain of what is. I turn to the Jewish prayer known as "kaddish"—which is, as Leon Wieseltier says, "not so much a praise of God as a prayer for the praise of God."

I pray for praise against all those *nevers* of death: Daniel will never drive up the driveway again in his red truck; Daniel will never again move in that easy athletic gait of his, in clothes that always seemed too large or impossibly rumpled; his wife, his mother, his brothers, and I will never see his charmed smile, which transformed his entire face and made everyone around him a participant in his happiness.

He will never.

I will never.

He and I are talking.

Then I am writing this down.

I

LAMENTATIONS (1)

I.

Grief is the *art*
(can it ever be called that?)
of starting over. Every morning
the same morning.

Every evening the same.
The light tipping above
the horizon, dipping below.

A day. Another day
of second thoughts. Another night
of *if only, what if, what else
could we have done?*

II.

Days, weeks, months, years,
all unpunctuated,
an endless run-on sentence
devoid of verbs, actions, time

and without any of
those little logic words—
although, just as, similarly, but—
that connect one thought to another,

grief's preference the childlike
and then, and then, and then,
as in my six-year-old son's journal
in which every day, every event,

that summer in New Hampshire
had exactly the same worth
and felt to him like one
endlessly repeating summer day

which he loved, but which now,
as I read through it,
as if involuntarily,
day-by-day-by-day coldly numbs.

III.

If *language is fossil poetry,*
as Emerson believed,
each word shuddering to life
in the instant it spoke

reality to its speaker,
the word I bore into being

(if only because I'd never fully
experienced it) was *heartsore*,

from the Old English,
heortsarnes—meaning "grief,"
meaning exactly what
it sounds like it means,

a soreness which is
not a metaphor for some ache
that can be cured
or will go away in time,

but a soreness always present,
the *what is now*
and now will always be
that returns you, involuntarily

or by choice, to the *what is not.*
A word that is almost a sentence
in itself, waiting for each
of us to complete it:

he is heartsore, she is heartsore,
I am heartsore.
Heortsarnes—that deep bruise
of sound born into word.

WALKING WITH DANIEL

I don't know why, other than to be
somewhere else, I walked and walked
after his death. I took him with me,

his name always in my mouth,
and always said three times,
Daniel, Daniel, Daniel—

sometimes with the exasperation of
how could you be gone, sometimes
with the horror of *where are you, Daniel*,

sometimes just a calling out to him,
as if, now that he was gone,
he could be anywhere.

All winter my voice
came out of my mouth involuntarily,
speaking to an empty road

that dipped and rose, speaking
as though he could hear me
or my words could stake a claim for him

in this world he'd left.
I said, *the beeches have hung on*
to their leaves all winter long,

as if to declare that,
until something new arrives,
the past will not be let go.

Or: *there's a fox on the hillside,*
the kinetic flow of its body
matching the curve of the hill.

I couldn't say how it recalled
his once limber gait.
I said, *the pond's iced-over*

and full of scratches,
February's gray days are piling up
like a car crash, the last dirty patches

of snow appear like
the chalked outlines of victims
in the woods. For months I talked

to him as if he were
beside me. I noted each thing
I saw, my mad attending

a kind of ritual to bring back
what had been lost.
Each day I walked to no end

but the day's, the dark darkest
at road's edge where I plodded
along under the trees, car horns

sounding their drivers' surprise
when their headlights found me,
a dark figure disoriented and alone.

A PAIR OF ROSEATE SPOONBILLS

Nothing brings on my need to talk
like your death, that murky silence into which
all my words fall and yet keep replenishing
themselves in dire need of second chances.

I can't keep from narrating my days to you,
as if you were beside me here,
looking with my eyes at whatever it is
I'm seeing—this pair of Roseate Spoonbills

at the moment. The contradictions
of their being would have amused you—
are they ugly or beautiful? A mockery of form
or a perfection of form itself?—that sunset flush

of their body's pink and red featherings
offset by paddle-like wooden spoons for a bill.
They stir the muck, trusting what
they can feel, the water too dark to see through

or shattered into little triangles of light
each time a breeze sails across the marsh.
Sometimes I lose myself in a kind of trance
as they swing their bills, stir the bottom,

repeat, repeat. It's not self-obliteration
or some magical escape I feel. If you can
believe me, when I'm talking with you,
I'm more alive, more here, even if I know

I'm doing all the talking. It's as if I want nothing
else than for you to see them—how elegant
and ungainly they are, those bills so excessive,
so casually strange, perfectly suited to their task

and yet so comical. You'd have a good laugh
at that. And you'd appreciate this moment—
the sun's matchtip of light has gone out
and, in its afterglow, the pair of spoonbills

have become shadows crossing
the marsh in a cooling breeze that began
on the opposite shore and now riffles over
the water's pink flush towards where I am.

AFTERLIFE

After my son died, I knew why
Jack Gilbert had to carry that box,
shifting its weight, but never
putting it down. Like him, I tired,
my son over two hundred pounds,
and too much for me to bear.
Once I thought I heard my son say,
"Put me down and let me be."
We had come to an empty beach,
and the tide was pulling away,
leaving an even vaster beach behind.

I sat for a long time, then lugged him
as far as a clearing in the woods.
I saw myself in a small clear pond.
I didn't look good. That's when
I heard my son again, who liked to chide me
in what he called my poetry voice,
give me the advice of a fortune cookie:
"Let the emptiness remain empty."
And then: "Stop writing down
everything you think I'm telling you.
This is your afterlife, not mine."

NOT A WISH

Be careful what you wish for,
my grandmother was fond of saying,
and certainly the stories we read together
confirmed her own experience—
no one ever wished for the right thing,
as if *that* choice were simply an impossibility,
connected to a human failing so deep and so ancient,
choosing wasn't a choice at all,
but only a guarantee for going wrong.

Even when my son was suffering, I held back
my wish for what I wanted most;
and after he died, I never asked for
my deepest wish to be granted,
as if part of me believed something
could go more wrong than already had.
Maybe once terror arrives at the door,
safety is all that matters, and not wishing
for safety, the safest way to assure it.

I still don't understand why I placed
the carved Zuni stone crow
I carried around in my pocket for years
inside my son's thick fingers just before

the casket was closed. I didn't think of the crow
as a guide in some afterlife. No, it wasn't
a plan or even a decision—just a last second
impulsive act, as if the crow would be
a better safeguard than anything
more reasonable I knew not to wish for.

AT THE CEMETERY

After my son's death, October leaves fell
on schedule. Wood smoke blew across a field.

I could find nothing to steer the days.
There was only the lifeless freedom

of my own helplessness. My future seemed
unendurable, and yet it had to be endured.

Now, I meet him at his grave.
A summer thunderstorm announces itself

in flashes and gusts of wind that rip leaves
from the maple tree beside his grave,

where, once again, I think of his birth.
Unplanned, at home, ten minutes from first pains

to his being here. Just like that, I feel him
rushing into my hands, the weight of him.

I think of this so I do not lose my fatherhood.
Now, as trees bend south to north in the cemetery,

and the storm approaches, *groaning* as St. Paul
says the world groans like a mother in childbirth,

I groan: Lord, grant me this fatherhood of pain,
do not let grief be finished with me,

if only because it gives birth to my dead son
who is both not here, and not not here.

LOCKET

You carry our son in a locket
you hang around your neck

each morning, a way, I guess,
of carrying what isn't and what is,

a past that must be kept
present even as the past recedes.

It circles your neck like the string
your mother tied to your finger

as a child for memory's sake,
though you don't need a reminder

to open the locket and let our son breathe,
even if his picture takes your breath away.

In the picture, he is bent over his phone,
his look mischievous, both dimples showing,

as if he's just sent off a sly, tongue-in-cheek
text to one of his brothers, or you.

I like the way you look in on him, opening
what you might have locked away,

even when each time the force of horror
meets head-on the force of your love,

and squeezes your eyes shut.

IN THE UNWALLED CITY (2)

ON AUGUST 18, 1986, my wife woke me from a restless sleep and announced that the time had come. This was not a planned home birth, but by the time my wife asked, "should I push or not," her water broke, and Daniel surfed out with such force that I can honestly say I caught him. I cleared the mucus from his mouth and watched him redden into life in my hands. He arrived in a hurry. And he hurried through life.

What made Daniel Daniel was his intensity. Yeats, in his poem "In Memory of Major Robert Gregory," once divided people into two categories—those that are like a banked fire, slowly burning through the night, and others who consume

> The entire combustible world in one small room
> As though dried straw, and if we turn about
> The bare chimney is gone black out
> Because the work had finished in that flare.

Daniel was definitely in the combustible category. He could work all day, then work again at night on a house he and Leisl had bought to rehab. He loved old houses and barns; he knew how they were constructed and how to make them sound and right once they had fallen into disrepair.

The morning Daniel died, I walked on a local road to slow my thoughts and gain the smallest foothold against the assault of my emotions. A neighbor and local contractor drove past me, then stopped, and backed up to where I was standing. He was an old, tough Swedish guy who had helped Daniel get some good work around town. He rolled down his window, said he had heard about my son's death. He was sorry. Then he said Daniel was a "good boy" who worked hard. He didn't know how that simple statement summed up Daniel's values, his outsized energies, his attack mode of work.

But it wasn't just a good work ethic that defined Daniel. He hungered for life. He was unafraid of those darkest questions we ask about life, and unafraid to exist in that in-between of believing that life had purpose and order, and that life was simply a random event, luck and randomness ruling each day.

I taught at the College of the Holy Cross for thirty-eight years. One of the greatest gifts and pleasures in my life was teaching Daniel, who took my course, The Bible and Literature. When he died, I asked Leisl for his college papers and notebooks. They are difficult for me to read, nearly impossible. But his thinking shines through. Writing about Abraham at Moriah, he did not see some easy story of Abraham's obedience and faith, but rather saw an altar where all rationality had to be sacrificed. He knew what it was like to arrive at a place where no amount of thinking could make sense of what was happening. He had known real losses.

I see again how intimately he understood Abraham's need to control, to think he could know what God wanted. He seemed to know intuitively that Abraham had to come to that place where thinking is useless, where all rational thought leads only to what is irrational. In his midterm exam, Daniel drew a connection between Abraham, Jacob, and Job. All three believe they have a hold on the world and that their thinking divides them from others. And they are right to some extent. But each thinks they can understand what God wants. Each confuses the world that makes sense in their own human terms with God's world. And each must have, as Daniel wrote, their world shattered.

When Daniel and I talked on the drive to and from Holy Cross, I tried to articulate my sense of life and my gratefulness for it. He would ask me to explain the use of the word "provide" in the Abraham and Isaac story or just what Joseph meant by "providence." If I spoke about "provide" meaning more than a ram in a thicket, that Yahweh had already provided a creation and the commandments and had promised in Exodus to provide for the Israelites' trek in the wilderness; if I spoke of Joseph's free will, of how "providence" didn't mean, "don't worry, God will make everything turn out okay"; or if I spoke of how God did not create Joseph's destiny, but rather Joseph, because of his experiences in the pit and with his brothers, participated in his destiny's unfolding, Daniel might nod in assent, and then wonder how our free will and God's will can work together. He knew the perversions of the human will. Or he might ask a question he knew would get to me: How does God's love accept that, for someone with mental illness, every day is a torture? How does God provide in that situation? At his funeral service, his uncle read from the hymn to Wisdom in Job: "Mortals do not know her path, nor is she to be found in the land of the living." Daniel's life swung between an ecstasy in being alive and the grief of not-knowing, of not finding that path to wisdom.

His death is a shattering of meaning. Don't misunderstand me—I never expected my son's death to have meaning. I mean only that death, suffering, grief—they truly collapse our house-of-cards rationality, all our self-deceitful ways of thinking we know what we do not know. We always know that truth, but we gradually bury it over and over, since it is impossible to live in that blown-open state of not knowing.

Grief is the practice of trying to make sense out of something which can never be made sense of. It brings us back to one of the basic truths of our existence: we are not in control. What we want to know so desperately remains outside our grasp, always. Mr. Ramsay, Virginia Woolf's philosopher supreme in her novel *To the Lighthouse*, admits he can only reason to "R" in the alphabet of knowing. Simone Weil said we must live on the cross of such contradictions.

I am trying.

II

LAMENTATIONS (2)

I am weary with my crying.
   —Psalm 65:5

Almost every day now, catalogues fill
The mailbox—clothes, shoes, sheets, fall

Bulbs for a burst of color next spring—
A bright world of ten thousand things

To buy, to say we are living, that we can be alive.
Buy a new Vitamix and, surely, we'll thrive.

And so we do. Amazon Prime saves us
Time and the regrets of waiting for this

Or that other item we don't need. We knew,
Didn't we, as we pushed Payment and Continue

And, finally, with only a slight hesitation, Accept,
The price we'd pay: this weeping over what

Does not suffice. Grief says the sky is never blue

Enough. Grief says weep and so we do.

***

Grief sets my wife down this afternoon,
Her heart a grave. She can't read,
Can't think, can't listen to music.
She's trying hard to remember
What she had planned to do today.

Grief sits with her on the couch,
Asks for a cup of tea and something
Sweet. The day is dark by four-thirty.
She sits under a lamp as if it were
The sun, drinking her tea with grief.

***

Daniel, whether you are
In some underworld,
Afterlife, or just the ground,

I am the same to you.
No father now,
Just a man turning back

To a past that had
A future, and crying
For death's amusement.

***

My wife weeps, I write—
What we have left
To fill the emptiness,
Neither very effective,

But all we have to help
Us go on loving what is
Gone, grief always
Ongoing, and going

Nowhere: tears that fall
And fall, but cannot fill
Even the basin of her
Hands, grief running

Through her fingers.
These words that keep back
Tears, but lack the means
Of transformation. Neither

Of us can change the state
Of things, which is to be
Bereft—her tears refuse
Song to keep our son nearby;

My words desire to become
Song, but cannot sing
Our son's return. A single task:
To keep him who's gone with us.

ICARUS

After our son died, my wife found him
in coincidences—sightings of hawks, mostly,
at the oddest of times and places, and then
in a pair of redtails that took up residence,
nesting in a larch above our barn, and how
their low, frequent sweeps just a few feet above us
before rising over our kitchen roof
made it seem as if they were looking in on us.
In a way, it all made sense, our son so at home
in high places—the edges of mountain trails,
walking on a roof, or later, after he became
a house painter, at the top of a forty-foot ladder.
So many mornings we woke to the redtails'
jolting screeches and, even if I was a casual believer,
their presence multiplied my love
for the ordinary more every day. We never thought,
of course, any of those hawks was our son—
who would ever want that? —but once,
watching one rise and rise on a draft of air,
I thought of Icarus soaring towards the sun—
as if an old story could provide the distance
I needed—waxed and feathered, his arms winged,
and remembered a babysitter's frantic call
to come home, immediately, after she'd found

our ten-year-old son nearly forty feet up
in an oak tree. I can almost hear him again, laughing
high up in the sky, throned on a branch,
his feet dangling, knowing nothing but the promise
of heights as he waved to me—
and I must have looked very small
calling up to him, staying calm
so falsely as I pleaded with him
to come down, to come down now.

LOST

Yesterday I said to someone,
I *lost* my son, as if a day would arrive
when I could find him. Even as I spoke,
I recognized my unrelenting desire
to see him and how it chokeholds

my days and nights. I did see him.
He was lying in the back yard.
Utterly still. I turned away from
the window, horror-struck
I had to see him dead once more.

But when I looked a second time,
I saw him lift himself up on one elbow.
Then he rose and walked
around the house. I ran outside.
He walked freely, unhampered

by the back pain he suffered
his last years. I held him and kissed
his cheek and neck. I wept.
I said his name, Daniel, Daniel.
Of course, I woke.

I tried again to find him in sleep,
but there was only the darkness
of my shut eyes. Night after night
after night, I've tried.
I cannot stop looking for him.

I think of him just before I lose myself
in sleep to influence my dreams,
and then again in the morning
when I find myself awake
and remember I have lost him.

BOBCAT

It came and went like a revelation and yet
was only a bobcat, and not the first
I'd seen cross the narrow field

behind my house to hunt for rabbits.
But this one just stood there in full daylight
as if it wanted to be seen, the sun turning

its tan coat gold, the bright October leaves
falling around it, or turning alertly in a breeze
against a background of cloudless blue sky.

From a window, I took the bobcat in
with binoculars—its tan coat slatted with
black bars, its erect black-tipped ears,

the off-white fur around its lips and chin,
and those yellow eyes with black pupils
that seemed to watch me as I watched,

freed for those two or three minutes from
the need to understand. I didn't ask how
the bobcat had come to be where it was,

and I to where I was, this first day of
my son's sudden death. It was October 14th,
and though I wanted to make the bobcat

what it was not—some type of offering or sign—
I simply watched it come and go,
though its strangeness has stayed with me:

a bobcat, incapable of sadness, and which
had no meaning, or none I could grasp,
stepped into the open and stood in leaf-fall

and afternoon's gold—not what
I would have asked for, but all that was
there, at home in the day's passing light.

ANOTHER STATE

I think of you in another state.
Another country. Another continent

where you are born again to others
who are your parents.

Or as if you slipped through some wormhole
into a parallel universe

where you live on a planet just like this one,
with the same parents, the same brothers,

the same wife, though everyone
has a different name.

In other words, never dead. Never nowhere.
Call it The Perpetual-State-of-the-Beloved

who lives in the world
of Never-To-Be-Found-Again.

These are the domains love opens
long past the hour when the grave closes

and death becomes
a starting point towards another state

where you've gone on
communicating something I cannot understand

or communicate myself—
something like light streaming in a room, almost alive,

almost as if, with the proper encouragement
from me, it could speak.

KOI POND: FAILED MEDITATION

I just wanted to sit, shut my eyes,
tilt my face to the sun, and try not to think,
but the koi, insistent, unappeasable,
crowded to my end, the water roiling
with their need, and, when I opened my eyes,
I saw them lift their bulbous heads,
making sounds with their rubbery, barbeled lips
as if they were gasping for air.

When I shut my eyes again
because I did not want to see, I saw
the little outdoor fireplace on my son's deck,
embers still burning. The October day
had not yet come into being,
the light anomalous, something between
night and morning. Inside, on the floor
of his living room, my son was dead.
His wife had waited with his body
until my wife and I arrived.

We lay next to him, touched his hair,
his forehead, his cheeks, his lips and chin—
and then I heard myself
trying to tell him we were there, we were

with him, we loved him,
but my words were more like moans
than words, every word sounding
its helplessness. When I opened my eyes,

there were the koi, their too-small pond
swirling with color—white, yellow,
black and white, gold, red and white—
all of them entangled, straining against
each other, mouths agape, turning
and turning in their net of water.

IN THE UNWALLED CITY (3)

DURING THE DAYS surrounding Daniel's death, as I walked around my house through the hours of the night, I spoke in a kind of babble, in a sentence untethered from syntax, from subject and verb. I nearly vomited words, not just the *No, No* of what shouldn't be, couldn't be, but irrevocably was, but the endless petitions that he be at peace, that my words—spoken, wailed, whispered—could help him (even though all my talking couldn't prevent his death) with his passage out of this world.

At times I got dressed and walked in the middle of the night, wandering aimlessly, as if I believed I might come upon someone or something that would help. Though Daniel was dead, I felt constantly the terror I had felt when Daniel was a teenager and still not home, the clock, seeming to shout again and again, that it was long after his curfew. Back then, I would walk from window to window looking for car lights. Or even drive around Woodstock, pointing a flashlight out the driver's side window as if I could find him. I checked sharp turns in the local roads, places where ground fog gathered, places I feared whenever my children drove off.

Where are you? my wife cried over and over into the darkness the night Daniel died. We cannot imagine our loved ones are nowhere. Or perhaps the question is simply "are you?" since it is oblivion, not location, we fear.

"We work in the dark," Henry James said. Grief is such work. What I write here is written in the dark, out of desperation—words that try to communicate something that was communicated by the death of my son and which I can never communicate.

Perhaps grief is an attempt to hit a note that would shatter this world like glass and allow me to walk through the barrier that keeps my son apart from me for all my remaining days.

Nothing new can happen between my son and me. And while I have taught the parable of the prodigal son many times, these days I feel not just why, when the lost is found, there is great cause for celebration, but how truly the zest goes out of life with such a loss. There is no word for the pairings of emotions one feels in grief—the enormity of love mixed with the enormity of sorrow.

Today, as I was writing this, Leisl sent photographs to my wife's phone. After Daniel died, she sold the house they had bought to fix up and either rent or sell once it was finished. The house was about three quarters finished. She sold it as is, but my wife, who finally relented on buying it ourselves (I didn't have the heart or the energy for the project), needed to give the new owners Daniel's plans for the unfinished parts of the house. One of the unfinished rooms, for which he had drawn a layout and bought appliances, was the kitchen. A chimney that took up a great deal of usable space had been dismantled and removed, a basement staircase had been moved, the ceiling had been vaulted, the 2x8 collar ties that ran from one outside wall to the other to keep the structure from bowing out had been boxed, but there were no cabinets, counters, or sink, and the subfloor waited to be covered with new wood boards. And today, incomprehensibly, Daniel's plans arrived, completed by the new owner, on my wife's cell phone. Everything was exactly in the places he had imagined it would go. The posthumous reality of that kitchen was like a letter arriving after the loved sender has died.

Near what turned out to be the end of Daniel's life, he was mostly house-bound, often even confined to bed. He suffered from terrible back pain and spasms, his granular discs often squeezing out between his vertebrae and pressing against the nerves that run down our spines.

My wife and I often drove over to his house to keep him company, reading books to him as he tried to find that one comfortable position in a chair. But this one day has stayed with me—it was going well (which meant our hours together had passed without conflict or that ill-at-ease feeling of existing as separate solitudes), and when I had finished reading and we had talked about a few pages of Erazim Kohak's *The Embers and the Stars*, I suggested he come back to our house for lunch. I had another plan in mind. On the way, I drove up the driveway of a house that was for sale in town. It had a good-sized barn and twenty or so acres of land. We just sat in the driveway between the gabled old farmhouse and the barn. The day was one of those perfect fall New England days—cloudless blue sky, leaves just turning on the trees or drifting down with the wind. We imagined the interior of the house, where walls could be removed to open up rooms, and we talked especially about the barn—how he would partition and arrange it to house his painting business. We never really believed for a second either one of us would buy the property, but we talked on and on about what we would do with it.

III

LAMENTATIONS (3)

The trailhead where the unimaginable began.

***

A tear in the fabric of this world
That does not reveal another.

***

The waiting for what has already passed
And cannot come again.

***

The daily recognition of the difference between
experience and memory.

***

All this want, not for what is, but for what is not.

***

What petrifies the hours of my days.

***

The abyss that opens between one day and the next.
My son is dead two years. He died yesterday.

**

My son and I are talking. Then his life is over
And I am writing this down.

**

My words—a filibuster without meaning or conclusion.

**

The ritual of trying to make sense where no sense is.

**

The sucker-punch of my own self-pity
As I lie in its caress.

**

Like being deaf to the applause of the sun clapping
Against the black and white cows in the field.

**

The way gratefulness still grates.

TORMENT AND LOVE

I asked God where my son was
and he said, you must choose—your son
or me, and, when I had made my choice,

I entered The-Place-Where-People-Go-On-Being,
and there was my son before me,
each hobbling step still spasming his back

and leg. Just as in life, all he wanted
was someone to believe him
when he told them the level of his pain.

As in life, whatever we thought we could do
for each other remained unspoken
amid all our speaking, though we kept at it,

because love wouldn't let us stop.
Again, my son looked at me as if I did not
have a clue, but tenderly. He asked

for more drugs to ease the pain. Again,
I refused. Our argument went on and on
in the Hell-Of-One-Track-Minds.

I wanted to wake from this irresolvable dream
and also to remain asleep, our torments bearable
because we were together again. Torment and love,

balanced on each side of the scale. Sometimes
our words seemed to mean what we hoped
them to mean and, just when I had started to believe

that even the ones most heated and barbed
had inside them a seed of resurrection,
I could feel myself coming to the surface

of sleep and, with one last backward look,
my dream lost, I sat up in bed
and found myself without a son, or God.

SWALLOWTAIL KITES

Another day of doing nothing, of nothing
to be done with this roiling sadness,

this restlessness that will not rest
after last night's rounds of sleep and waking

and my strange, involuntary calling out to you,
my lost one, in a voice almost unrecognizable.

And now I'm walking my over-eager dog
at the sunset hour, Florida cooling down,

the reprieve of a good-natured day slowing
to its end in calming pinks and yellows.

I've been watching a pair of swallowtail kites
glide by in elegant, effortless flight,

circle higher up, then downglide by again,
as if they've taken an interest in me.

But it's insects they're after, that generate
their improvisations with the wind,

their forked tails tilting left then right
as they snap an insect out of air

and eat on the wing. That's fine by me—
I'm lost in their wheeling and sloping maneuvers,

so intent on the next time they'll zip close-by,
I miss my dog squatting, then pulling at her leash,

wanting to move on to the next grassy smells,
to do what dogs do, and not this standing still,

looking at the sky and this pair of kites
as if they could steady me just as they steady

themselves in the wind with their tuning-fork tails.
But now my dog tugs hard,

and I'm off again, into what the night will bring.

MELANCHOLY'S MIRROR

In the shadowland of my room
this warm winter late afternoon, I watch a stinkbug
cross my wall. Also: two flies that woke this morning
and now, dazed, bump up against the windows.
I'd like to say I'm getting by and getting on with life,
but the latter is a stretch. A tapeworm of grief
has been eating my insides, eating the spirit
of who my son was, his lively mind, his courage
to accept the darkest contradictions.

I've sat here for hours, my companions these two
thoughts—my son is dead and done with me;
how can I know what my son's life was to him,
and him alone? If I set up a mirror on my desk, I'd see
a cartoon of hurt and lethargy. Just before
the stinkbug arrived, I was staring at Dürer's *Melancholia*
on my computer screen. All those tools—saw, plane,
hammer, calipers, ruler—like my son's, piled up now
in my garage waiting for me to do something with them.

And yet here I sit, as if I were tied up
like my neighbor's dogs. If I were a dog, I'd howl
all day like them. I embarrass myself.
Why can't I remember what ridiculous luck

it is to be alive? One of those flies just buzzed
in front of my face, as if to say,
"Where have you been hiding yourself?"
I could ask the same question, but now
it's on my nose, daring me to come alive. . . .

I belong today to my own anatomy of melancholy—
its long wait for what never happens.
Its shut-down of the future. Its after-
knowledge of death that knows no more
than it did before. Its inability to complete
a life that simply ended. Dürer's figure,
winged but paralyzed, moping, tools spread
before him, but unable to create. These words
that lurk like insects this winter late afternoon.

AUBADE

When we turn off the lights,
and my body takes the shape of yours
as if I could quell what is inside you,

I cannot hold you tight enough to quiet
whatever wild and untamable thing
has entered your body.

The doctor wanted to prescribe pills
(you refused immediately) to prevent
this nightly recurrence of shudders.

Three years and counting, and if I dread
our nightly ritual, I've come to love you more
for the way you store up each day's pains

then let some go throughout the night,
as if you sense that to be free of these jolts
of grief would mean losing our son again.

I sometimes count the hours to sunrise.
Then the sun's lozenge of orange becomes
an antidote to the night's weight.

I like to sit on our bed and look at you,
last night's thoughts put to rest for the time being.
Soon you'll take on the sorrow that returns

with waking. But for now, you bear the peace
of sleep's thoughtlessness, and—forgive me
for saying so—you seem a mother to no one.

DOVES IN FOG

Six a.m. and nothing here but fog
and the weakest of sun-gods
trying to scissor the fog into pieces,
a little blue patch here, another there.
Then gone, the windows completely misted,
making shadows of whatever flies by outside.
I am sitting with my sorrow
and a cup of tea behind these windows.
I'm waiting to see the pair of doves
I have been listening to as if they are
some type of meditative exercise
to focus myself on the present moment.

I like being unable to see, and I like
forgetting myself, if only for a brief time,
when I'm taken up by the doves' call
and response—insistent, relentless—
in the live oak I know is outside my window.
My son has been dead nearly three years.
I still cannot see the doves, or the tree,
except for its charcoal-like outlines.
Most likely I am hearing my own sadness
in the doves' tiresome moans.

Two palm trees, visible just this moment,
shake out the morning's dampness in the first breeze
as if their raspy rattle can clear my day.
But the doves, with their clerical collars
and their *who, whoo-whoo*, keep up their inquiry,
not letting go of that old question: just who is
sitting here, custodian of an empty mug,
whoever he once was now someone else,
holding on to what is gone, the collared doves
flying off as the fog lifts and another
Florida day, exactly like yesterday, heats up.

SKETCHBOOK: NAPLES, FLORIDA

The royal palms bathe in the soft warm air
of February and everywhere I look there is the play
of glittering afternoon light—on store windows
and metal bistro tables, on the well-polished
always white Mercedes and Lexuses, on the sorbet
pinks and oranges and lime greens of faux-Spanish
buildings. The most ordinary things here seem
make-believe, outside of time, like images projected
on a screen and, for now, this Lotus-land
of ease and assurance serves my hazy recollections
of contentment, my need to push away death,
even if its reminders are everywhere—
in consignment shops lining the highways,
and, here, on Fifth Avenue where the aptly titled
Provident Jewelers keeps buying up
the best silverware, china, and jewelry of
the newly dead. For now let this be
another piercingly blue day in Florida,
clear as a mirror unstained by reflection.
Let the live oaks translate the breezes off the Gulf
and let the idle days pile up like cocktails
at Happy Hour, and strollers in twos and threes
mosey in and out of street-side boutiques
and restaurants, content with the intricate evasions

of shopping and the driest white wines.
I'll have another gin and tonic and act as if
I'd stumbled into someone else's reassuring dream
where any minute now my dead son will stop by
for a drink with me and, together, we'll watch
the sun dawdle on the horizon of the Gulf,
this day sketched by sunlight on the threshold of dying.

IN THE UNWALLED CITY (4)

MEMORIES—SO MANY people say, "you'll always have your memories." But even though my son died almost three years ago, memories of him are almost entirely painful. They are not Wordsworthian "recollections in tranquility," but sharp stabbing pains that arise out of nowhere. Triggered by some sappy pop song or a commercial about back pain on TV, memories of Daniel torpedo me when I am least prepared. They never miss their target. First, there is the utter pain of memories; then the horror of remembrance which feels too often like a form of forgetting, of losing sight of Daniel's features, the way his mouth curled wryly when he said something deadpan and funny, or the way, when he rested, he sprawled, he basked, his muscled body went limp. "The Walrus," my brother called him, humming the Beatles' song.

I try instead to accept that Daniel is alive. I am not delusional, nor am I denying his death. I do agree with Anne Carson: "I have to say this person is dead, but I don't have to believe it." I have to say Daniel is dead, but I don't have to live as if he is. In Wordsworth's poem "We Are Seven," the poem's speaker comes upon a "simple child," who, when asked about her family, says they are "seven in all." The speaker learns that two siblings have died, but when he asks the expected question, how, then, can your family be seven, the little girl responds: "Their graves are green, they may be seen." She tells the man she knits her stockings by their graves, hems her kerchief, and sings songs to them. When the man insists that they must be five since two are in heaven, the little maid replies, "O Master! We are seven." Her siblings are alive to her even if they lie buried in the churchyard. And, Wordsworth suggests, why shouldn't the little girl's siblings live on in her love for them? Perhaps the little girl possesses a wisdom we have lost by following too directly the path of what is rational and makes sense: seven minus two is indeed five as the girl's interlocutor insists.

I am seventy. My son is not here any longer. And he is not not here. I don't eat my supper at the cemetery where he is buried. But if I am asked, how many children do I have, I still answer, three. If pressed about where they live and what they do, I have no trouble saying one of my sons has died, that he lived in Woodstock his whole life, and loved the town and area. He married his high school sweetheart who still lives and works nearby. He loved old houses and ran his own painting business.

But the answer can only be three. I don't ever say to someone I had three sons, but one of them died. Am I trying to cut off their sympathy, even pity, I know will follow such a statement? I don't think so. The truth is the dead go on living in our lives.

I do say—if only to my wife and close friends—I can, at times, feel Daniel's presence. Such a strange word—it can mean the fact that someone is in a place; or it can refer to the feeling that someone is still in a place although they are not there or are dead. But I mean something else. That Daniel is alive in more than my grief. What does saying such a thing mean? In part it means his presence makes a claim on me, even if it is beyond my ability to understand it. I certainly don't mean I feel his presence in this or that room or at this or that specific time—what the philosopher Gabriel Marcel referred to as a "vaporized object."

I could simply say that I have had the experience of Daniel becoming part of me. And that would be partly true. But, when I speak about Daniel's presence, it is something more. I experience it as a calling forth of something in me, some way of meeting it, even "answering" to it. I often hear his voice, though it is usually saying something like, "Stop writing down the things you think I'm saying." His presence, which is mostly felt as the pain of his absence, nevertheless has a "hereness" which defies logic: Daniel is emphatically not here in precisely the way I would most desire—in a solid and tangible body. And yet.

Soon after he died, I found myself narrating my days to him—I'd say a red-shouldered hawk that's nested down by the barn just swept in above the patio, as if it were looking in on your mother and me as we grilled hamburgers, its *kee-year, kee-year,* coming close, then fading into the distance. When I walked, I acted as if he were beside me, noting, as if to him, the first appearance of the lily pads that would choke the pond in a month's time. I was that little maiden in Wordsworth's poem, and I lived in a kind of perpetual present in which he was both alive and dead.

I know now that there was a purposeful illusory dimension to that constant narration of events. I could not, I would not give up my fatherhood. I even prayed for the continued pain of my son's absence.

The first summer after Daniel died, I was teaching on Whidbey Island, off the coast north of Seattle. My wife and I went off one day to find two potters who advertised their pottery as oven and stove-top safe. Their business was in the middle of the woods, and their isolation suited the two women just fine. As we talked, and then bought a baking dish, giving them our address, our area code immediately registered with them. Their business had first started in Chaplin, Connecticut, which was just down the road from us. We even knew the street where it had been. And now here we all were, talking as if we knew one another for years, on the other side of the country.

As we returned to our car, we noticed some small, clay, hand-built, church-like buildings made to house votive candles. The woman who made them called them *spirit houses*. Usually such a name would have sent me running to our car. I'm much more the meatloaf/bread baking dish kind of person than the votive candle lighting kind. So is my wife. But we paused over one we both liked, then bought it and had it shipped home. When we returned from the northwest, it was waiting for us.

To be honest, I didn't know what to do with it. My wife set up the Scandinavian-looking church on an old English pine chest in our kitchen with a picture of our son behind it. She's lit a votive candle in it each morning and the smell of the match and, after, the candle burning, travels to my study, just off the kitchen. At family gatherings, she sets it on the dining room table.

Neither of us think this little church houses our son's spirit. In fact, that idea was so ludicrous to me at first, I ignored the little church in the kitchen. But now I visit it when I take a break from writing or reading, when a wash load needs to be moved to the dryer, when I make a cup of tea. I stand before it and look at Daniel. And most days, he is more than simply a photograph. In the picture, he is bent over his phone, his look mischievous, both dimples showing, as if he's just sent off a sly, tongue-in-cheek text to one of his brothers, or to my wife (I can't imagine it's to me since I don't use a cell phone).

Who am I visiting?—I'd answer, my son, who's become part of my daily rounds, part of my day. Some days I touch his face as if he were alive and break down, but most days I just look at him and think of him watching me make a cup of tea or carefully folding his laundry that he would never put away. Or I don't imagine anything at all, just sense the candle burning, or look at the clay church glowing on the chest in the middle of another gray day. In a few hours, it goes out. Tomorrow, my wife will light it once again. It's a way, at least for now, of sanctifying time, of making—if we are there to meet him—Daniel's life a continuous present.

These words from the gospel of John have lodged in my mind: "Nevertheless I tell you the truth; It is expedient for you that I go away: for if I go not away, the Comforter will not come unto you; but if I depart, I will send him unto you." Jesus is speaking to his disciples. And, presumably, the disciples' reaction would have been something like Ben Jonson's "O could I lose all father now." How can this nebulous Comforter replace the living and breathing Jesus who walks and talks and drinks wine with them? And what kind of deal is this: if I don't go away, then no Comforter? Not a deal that makes rational sense. Not a deal anyone would choose. But a deal Love offers perpetually, and we can refuse or accept.

Don't get me wrong. I don't think Daniel is sending me the comfort of the Holy Spirit. But I am saying, I have had some sense of the Comforter these past years. When I say I feel the presence of my son, I am saying—at least it feels this way to me—that Christ's death and resurrection is both a one-time event and a perpetual event, the way each year the Christmas hope is that Christ is born in us anew. Christ's going away involves his resurrection first in Mary, and then in his disciples. And then in us. His going away, his absence even, is found now in the comfort of my son's continued rebirth in my life. I feel like my role is to conceive my son over and over. This is not some desperate task of a grieving father, but rather a belief in the ritual of remembrance. Christ's death is an act of love; it completes the story of Yahweh who tells the Israelites, "I will walk with you and be your God." Now Christ says I will suffer as you suffer, die as you die. And when I die, I will send the Comforter to you.

I am saying that Daniel goes about my day with me. But how?—the comfort is not so much the promise of life after death, but rather the possibility that there can be life-in-death-in-life. Perhaps love is as strong as death, as the Song of Solomon asserts. I know love is what goes on in death. I am always my son's father. He is always my son.

IV

NOVEMBER DEER

This morning I think of myself
as the fog that has made the entire world
outside my windows disappear
and, for a time, I live enjoyably
inside the fog's featureless comfort,
as if there is nothing to dwell upon
or anyone to miss—and then, three deer
are right outside the window
where I am standing out of sight,
their bodies wrapped in scarves of fog.
They have so suddenly appeared
it feels as if they have always been right here,
dipping down and lifting up
their long necks, nosing this or that apple
as if there is some absolute difference
between the ones they choose
and the ones, at least for now, they don't.
They have a calm alertness, always poised
for what might happen next—
a readiness impossible to imagine—
as their teeth crush the apples
into pieces, and their long, thick tongues
lick the juices from their lips
as if they are savoring the taste,

though this may only be my projection,
my imagination wanting to keep pace
with the richness of this morning scene,
this collage of grays and browns
punctuated by the redness of the apples,
my delight nearly palpable,
and yet, even as I say so, lost,
the deer disappearing inside the woods,
the woods disappearing inside the fog,
and the sadness I'd let the fog erase
rushing back into the room.

FATHER'S DAY

Your two brothers have come
to comfort your mother and me, and we do
what we do, have done—visit you
in the cemetery. We sit on the stone wall
or on the grass, inmates of our grief.
Our bodies leave us little choice
but to sigh or weep, the pain newborn.
What else but to invite it in.
We sit until we feel you buried inside
each of us, then return home.

I won't be alive when you are dead
the thirty-one years you lived. I can still
bring you back, voice and all, and practice
each day, beginning with your childhood.
My eyes shut, my head bowed,
I am a monk and this remembering,
the stations of devotion,
a feeling for the state of those first feelings
that became a mere memory—
the love that may remain and live after death.

After, we eat. We make a toast to you.
We light a votive candle in the little clay church

the potter called a *spirit house.*
We don't try to summon you
and no one's expecting you to show,
but it's nice to sit here in the dark
with the candle flickering inside
the church, like—*Christ, just say it*—
like your spirit coming and going in our minds
as the night darkens around a half moon.

AUGUST

The name of the dog my son left behind,
a black English Labrador with a big square head
and muscled chest, always nose down in search of food.
August—named for all those events that now give pain:
my son's birthday, his wife's, their wedding anniversary.
Still she wags her tail and head, has no memory
of my son, who one day was there, and then not,
and would love him once again if he simply turned up
these three years later. Strange how he keeps on
coming back to life and then dying each time August
visits and stranger still my need to say something
even about his dog, her black coat lush and glowing
in the afternoon light that tumbles down
as I pet her and she lets me, waiting impatiently
for me to finish up my meal and make a small offering
of my plate. August—still so much the same
as when he was alive, so lovable and goofy,
anything but august, but hallowed all the same.

ST. FRANCIS OF THE BIRD FEEDER

Time has dawdled away and nothing
I had planned to do has gotten done,
and here I am standing at the window again,
the dim winter light and gray stone of sky
dulling the white of fallen snow. Birds wing
back and forth to the feeders I've hung
from a metal pole with arms—chickadees,
titmice, nuthatches, downy woodpeckers—
and I'm looking into that circle of fluttering birds
when the disc of faintly glowing sun
behind the pole reminds me of the halo around
St. Francis's head in Giotto's painting of him
preaching to the birds, love holding them
in a wheel of flight around him
or lining them up on the ground like these juncos
pecking for fallen seed. And when I take it all
a step further, wondering if St. Francis
could show these poor birds the kingdom,
my dead son's voice breaks in,
perfectly clear, and exactly as I remember it,
mocking my need to turn a metal pole
into St. Francis. He's gotten a laugh out of me,
and lightened, if only a bit, the weight of the day,
even if I've already turned back to the pole

where a pair of cardinals rest on St. Francis's arm,
and I wait, hoping to hear his voice again.

NEXT

It's as if I've woken in another life,

recognizable but so completely altered, so changed,
it's as if I am standing next to myself

in a place where the days go by, seasons change,
but always without arrival and passage.

This day is locked in clouds without a door
for the sun to enter. I am standing next to

my son's grave, imagining myself looking at
my son's grave.

How long must I stand in this cemetery
reading from its library of fallen maple leaves?

Or lose myself to the dusty sparrows
disappearing inside the secret evergreens?

Or keep faith with the oracles of crows?
I am here with my son who is here and not here.

How long before I can stand in his absence
and not be absent myself,

before I can be here like one of those Chinese poets
calmly watching the geese wing overhead,

noting only a cool day, no sun,
the yellow-gold maple leaves floating down.

COFFIN PHOTOS

I'm listening to the undiminished
soft exhale of snow falling into water,
and to the water, nearly motionless,
softly lapping against the sides
of an anchored dug-out canoe.
Time pauses in the slow falling of snow,
every moment exactly the same
as the one before. The canoe is empty
and its emptiness stays with me,
like someone's absence. The head
of a stylized bald eagle, its take-it-all-in
eye too large for its head, is carved
mid-canoe, just above the waterline,
its wings raised along the entire length
of the canoe's side, the eagle vigilant
above that pair of huge, oaring wings.

All morning, exhausted by the weight
of doing nothing, I have been looking,
on and off, at this woodcut of the canoe
on my wall, moving between
daydream, grief, and remembrance.
I bought it in a gallery in Tofino,
on Vancouver Island, my son, his wife,

and my wife mocking my purchase,
or rather, my preoccupation with death,
which the empty canoe symbolized.
We took photographs of ourselves
posed against towering rocks that leaned
into the emptiness at low tide,
or on rocky outcroppings with backdrops
of wind-twisted pines, gray beach,
distant blue and white tumbling waves.

Seventy, I joked about how
the photographs, once I died,
would be pinned on those poster boards
that try to bring the dead back into the world
of the living. Or to give mourners something
to talk about as they wait to stand before
my casket. Or perhaps I thought
I could order the future. Six months later
it was my son who died. He hardly appears
in the photographs we took. He's always
just outside of the frame, stretching
face down on the path we're on,
his back spasming. Or huddled in pain
against a rock as we walk this or that beach.

Now three years from his death,
I find him this morning where he is not—
in that empty canoe. When I shut my eyes,
I can hear the snow again being extinguished

by the water. I can hear a raven's crawk
and the creaking trunks of snow-laden trees.
I can taste the salt in the air and I hear
the ocean in the swells of a breeze;
and I can feel the canoe rocking
in the cove where it seems to belong,
as if this is its proper place, anchored
in this woodcut's snowy afterlife.

AN ANSWER WITHOUT
A QUESTION

If he were alive, he might have shrugged
and said, *things happen for no reason,*
but he wasn't, he was only my son
in a dream, where he found me
sitting in the woods trying to understand
his death. There were birds I knew
but no longer had names for,
and a half-dozen deer browsed nearby
as if I was not there. I was so happy
to be speaking with my son,
but, in the middle of what I was saying,
he disappeared. I kept sitting where I was,
as if he'd return again, but I knew
nothing else was going to happen.
When I woke, I had that feeling
I often have when getting into bed
of both dread and the possibility of relief.
I was still partly in the dream, and I felt
he was like a god, utterly removed,
and not knowable any longer.
Shaking, I sat up and tried to focus on
the larches outside feathering the wind,

and a sliver of moon that caught and released
a scrim of fast-moving clouds. I breathed in
the smell of the grass I'd mowed
that afternoon, then rolled towards my wife
whose skin was cool to my touch. Far off
in the woods, I heard the sense-startling
yips and bawls of a pack of coyotes.
All of it came to me in a wave of sensations
nothing like words and yet, oddly, felt
like a gift, something like an answer.

EARLY SPRING

During the time I could not bear to see
the farmlands and red barn
(my son's handiwork) that once gave joy
as I passed, there came a moment
when, car windows down, my eyes watering,
I was overtaken by the raw, rank smell
of manure being sprayed in great arcs.

I stopped my car, laughed out loud, thought:
it's the Lord giving me shit. And shit,
to my surprise, was just what I needed—
its ebullience, its transport, its pungent energy
working its conversions—
dead grass, shit, new grass, cows, milk.

It seemed as if the grass had agreed to some plan
to lie low for a time and then spring up,
to let this caramel spring rain of manure
balance the books, the something always ending
with the something always beginning
(though even then I knew the death of these fields
was nothing like the death of my son).

Still, the insects suddenly here again
swirled above the fields, and great clouds
of starlings flung themselves into air,
braided together, and then flew into a roadside oak
like leaves in a sped-up tape of spring.
And I sat, breathing deeply, taken over by

the earthly tang of the spirit moving over the fields.
The barn glowed in the late sun like the ending
of a bad movie. I imagined the soon-to-be grass
growing in the dark, and the returning geese
pecking at the first shoots and, finally,
the cows lumbering back to the barn full of milk—
and I said, *Shit* to that, with gratitude and praise.

SCREENSAVER

Sure, every photograph is an elegy
to what was, but this photograph—
which I've turned into my screensaver—
of my son has him suspended in mid-air,
both rising and falling. He has just jumped
from a rocky outcropping thirty feet above
the shimmering water of Lake George
that flashes silver and gold.
The day itself is glittering with light
that has the feeling of being
excessive, and there are (I've counted)
seven different shades of green
in the hemlocks and cedars and white pines
growing from the rocky soil of the island.
My son is alive in the thrill of his airborne body,
though it is quiet in the photograph,
no cheers and whoops from his friends
who are waiting at the top to jump,
no sounds of the boats idling below or the waves
sloshing against their bobbing hulls.
I will not see him cleave the surface of the lake
and vanish with hardly a splash
and then break back into the light,
silvery water cascading from his hair and shoulders.

And I will not see him climb back up the rocks,
eager and intent on his next single-second flight.
But almost daily I give thanks
for this moment in which the past is gone
but never dead, this glimpse
of the terrible sorrow to come, but also
of something like an afterlife
in which his body, relaxed, calm, hovers
as if it's forgotten its heaviness,
the air holding him fast, halfway between
two places at once, the good light of sky
and the ease of bright water that waits.

QUASSET AND SPRUCEDALE

My son died, but I always think of him as here.
Unsure these days of my purpose and place,

I come to this little country cemetery, the dependable
seasons arriving and departing—freshly cut lawn,

falling leaves, snow, and then all those various
light greens of spring. It's spring now. In my mind,

my son cannot be nowhere, and yet I cannot imagine
where he is, except here, growing older inside me

as I grow older, more and more aware that the life he had
has become mine, or at least mine to live out or caretake

as best I can, even as my own death nears.
And so I come here, where I, too, will be buried

in this newly purchased family plot, the two of us,
or, more accurately, our headstones, side by side,

tilting into time in the East Quasset Cemetery,
the spring rush of water surging over the dam

and then under the one-car bridge where Quasset Road
meets Sprucedale, that diagonal, hardly used

brookside road we both loved to drive along.

THE WORDS WE SPEAK

Because we have been married for nearly forty years,

There's a language we both speak, often thinking

The same thought at the same time, or finishing

The other's sentence. But, lately, when we speak

Of our grief, sometimes the very same words

Mean something different to each of us.

Or we find ourselves searching for words

That do not exist, or are simply inadequate

At naming those moments of sorrow so great

We can barely breathe. Still, we have begun

To speak of what, despite those differences,

Is shocking but common to us both—how

The naked openness of our feelings in grief

Has returned us to an intimacy like the one

We felt with our newborns. There's a raw tenderness

Between us now in the words we speak

At the end of our day, as if we were both writing

To our dead son, even as we allow ourselves

To be sealed in sleep, like an envelope

Placed in the mailbox, flag up, an envelope

With two different love letters inside.

IN THE UNWALLED CITY (5)

MY SON DIED OF AN accidental drug overdose. He was addicted to pain medication, and he had had one back operation that failed and was scheduled for another in two weeks when he died. In fact, my wife, Leisl, Daniel, and I had a conference call with the surgeon from Mass General the very morning he died. In time, his back problems would most likely have been solved—a fusion was in the future for sure, though surgeons thought that having one at such a young age would probably weaken other discs and create the need for two or three more fusions in the future.

But Daniel's *now* was unbearable. We often hear people say, "live in the moment." In many ways, pain, ironically, is a total living in the present moment. The future doesn't exist. The past feels long lost. The present is all there is and that present is nearly unbearable pain. I remember my wife doing a mindfulness meditation from *Full Catastrophe Living*. When the meditation was over, she asked Daniel what thoughts had come to him. He said, "only thoughts of pain, where it was located exactly and how I could adjust my body to lessen it."

I do not blame the surgeons that worked with him. I confess I have real hatred for Purdue Pharma and the corporate greed that so casually trumps human life. And for the medical world's belief that pain killers, though they were not ideal, were still the best possible solution for pain, even when most doctors freely admit that the understanding between the mind and bodily pain is an utter mystery and that MRIs clearly cannot give them an image of what someone is suffering. And I do not blame Daniel. He had the strongest of wills. But the pain he felt day after day, year after year, without relief, wore him down.

Two years after he died, my neck started spasming in severe pain. I couldn't stop the spasms, which came about four or five seconds apart. The pain was physical—my brain sending false signals to my nerves—but it almost felt psychological, as if I needed to experience what my son experienced the last two years of his life. Two days into my pain, I would have agreed to anything—shoot me full of heroin but take this pain away. I understood at that moment what Daniel suffered and how pain becomes a demon inside one's head that runs rampant and must get what it needs. I would have taken anything to alleviate the bodily pain and to escape my own shouting brain.

I have often thought about our conversations on Daniel's back deck the last year of his life. Our subject was often drugs: how he believed he needed more pain medication, how I pleaded for him to lessen what he took each day. We argued, both enraged and with a kind of calm, steely rationalism. Daniel more than held his own. In the lulls between arguing, I'd tell him how much I loved him, and beg him, "Just let me in, I feel like you're holding something back."

I'm sure he lied more than once about his drug intake, and that part of what he held back was what he didn't want me to know. Shame makes expert liars of us all. Often we just sat together, elsewhere but just a few feet apart in our chairs, ill-at-ease in our separate solitudes, both wanting our hours to pass without conflict and yet feeling that conflict just beneath the surface of everything we said. He sensed my yearning and at times would look at me with both disdain and sympathy, as if he felt sorry for me, as if my desire for him to open up to me were so far beyond possible I was a fool for asking.

During the last year of Daniel's life, my wife and I did a year-long version of the Ignatian Spiritual Exercises. I love the Exercises, especially for the way they bring me back to a posture of gratitude. I feel the same about the Psalms.

But pain and grief can't help but find the *grate* in gratefulness; some days, being grateful can actually grate on me. Why? I am still thankful—for my life, for Daniel's life. I am thankful, surely, for the fullness of the love Daniel knew in Leisl, and in her and our family's love for him. And I am thankful for the love Daniel knew through his friends and for those mentors and teachers who taught him with the example of their actions and lives. I don't feel as if he was cheated out of more life, though I think of him each day, and how he'd enjoy this meal, or a Sunday's Patriots game, or that crystalline sky, or just something funny his brother said. And if I go somewhere new, I think always of what he would or wouldn't like about that place. But that's just how it is now, and how it will be. What grates, I think, is my stunted capacity to be grateful.

I get mired in my own thoughts: How desperately Daniel wanted to be healed—why couldn't I help him? What grates is that Daniel savored life, and then it became bland and repetitive—another day of not being able to work, another day of pain. My plight is no different from so many others. Two of my wife's sisters have lost children. Two of my closest friends have lost a child. Someone is dying of Covid-19 almost every minute. And all over the world, people die horrible deaths for no reason, victims of crime, war, ethnic cleansing, territorial and political disputes, and so on.

I had a dream in which Daniel said to me, "Just let life bring you back to life." I heard his voice perfectly. He is right of course. Grief desires not what is, but what is not. And joy cannot exist without gratefulness, without that casual astonishment of just how warm the russet-brown is on a towhee's side, and how the color is made warmer, offset by the towhee's black and white. Or how, now in spring, the towhee has changed its song, lifting its bill into the air and trilling, *drink your tea, drink your tea.*

I'm bringing back one of those days on Daniel's deck. We had given up reading from *Full Catastrophe Living* and bypassed yet another meditative exercise. I said let's just close our eyes and listen to what we hear. There was the sound of locust leaves shaking in the wind above his barn. And louder, the leaflets of ash that lined one of his property's boundary lines. A car and then a truck came towards us and faded away. We could hear a plane out of Hartford, heading north, high overhead. When we opened our eyes, we looked at the border ashes and their fringe of leaves against the sky where the silence of huge cumulus clouds drifted with the wind in a kind of procession. There was nothing to understand, but all our senses felt opened and we were floating, not long, just a few minutes at best, before we returned to the world where his back and legs still spasmed.

But we had felt the mercy and renewal we needed. We felt grateful. We didn't give thanks. We didn't need to: when we looked at one another again, each of us could have said with Jacob, "Your face is like the face of God to me."

Acknowledgments

Grateful acknowledgment is made to the following journals, in which these poems and essay were first published, sometimes in a slightly different version and with a different title:

Agni Review: Melancholy's Mirror

Anglican Theological Review: Early Spring

American Journal of Poetry: Walking

The Common: Sketchbook: Naples, Florida; Screensaver

Hampden-Sydney Review: Next

The Hudson Review: A Pair of Roseate Spoonbills

Image: Locket; Quasset and Sprucedale; In the Unwalled City (as a single essay)

New Ohio Review: Icarus (reprinted in *Poetry Daily*); An Answer Without a Question; Koi Pond: Failed Meditation; Doves in Fog

Pensive: The Words We Speak

Poetry Northwest: Bobcat

Southern Poetry Review: November Deer; Father's Day; August

The Southern Review: St. Francis and the Birdfeeders; Coffin Photos

Spiritus: Another State; At the Cemetery; Lamentations (1); Lamentations (2); Lamentations (3); Lost; Not a Wish

Tar River Poetry: Afterlife

Terrain: Swallowtail Kites

upstreet: Torment and Love

The poem "Screensaver" was awarded a Pushcart Prize.

I'm especially grateful once again to Jeffrey Harrison and William Wenthe, whose attention and skill have made so many of these poems better. And, finally, to Mark Burrows, editor of *Spiritus*, who believed enough in some of these poems to devote an issue of the magazine to them. And finally to my wife, Colleen, who has lived and suffered this book alongside me.

This book was set in Albertan, originally designed in 1982 as a metal-cut font by the distinguished Canadian type designer, Jim Rimmer, founder of Pie Tree Press. It was later digitized and released by Canada Type.

This book was designed by Shannon Carter, Ian Creeger, and Gregory Wolfe. It was published in hardcover, paperback, and electronic formats by Slant Books, Seattle, Washington.

Cover photograph by Nick Bolton on Unsplash.

CPSIA information can be obtained
at www.ICGtesting.com
Printed in the USA
BVHW032040090123
655867BV00023B/574